CW00695018

1 MONTH OF FREE READING

at

www.ForgottenBooks.com

By purchasing this book you are eligible for one month membership to ForgottenBooks.com, giving you unlimited access to our entire collection of over 1,000,000 titles via our web site and mobile apps.

To claim your free month visit:
www.forgottenbooks.com/free1241836

ISBN 978-0-428-52918-5
PIBN 11241836

environmental assessment
development concept plan
august 1982

SEQUOIA / KINGS CANYON
LODGEPOLE VALLEY

SEQUOIA / KINGS CANYON NATIONAL PARKS / CALIFORNIA

ENVIRONMENTAL ASSESSMENT/

DEVELOPMENT CONCEPT PLAN

LODGEPOLE VALLEY

SEQUOIA/KINGS CANYON NATIONAL PARKS

CALIFORNIA

U.S. Department of the Interior/National Park Service

CONTENTS

PURPOSE OF AND NEED FOR THE ACTION   1

AFFECTED ENVIRONMENT   3
    Existing Conditions   3
    Natural Environment   3
        Geology   3
        Soils   7
        Water Resources   7
        Vegetation   7
        Wildlife   7
        Endangered or Threatened Species   8
        Air Quality   8
    Visitor Use and Experience   8
        Visitation   8
        Visitor Experience   9
        Scenic Quality   9
    Cultural Environment   9
        Prehistory   9
        History   10

ALTERNATIVES   11
    Alternative A--The Proposed Action   11
    Alternative B   11
    Alternative C   11

ENVIRONMENTAL CONSEQUENCES   15
    Consequences Common to All Alternatives   15
    Alternative A--The Proposed Action   15
        Impacts on the Natural Environment   15
        Impacts on Visitor Use   16
        Impacts on the Cultural Environment   17
    Alternative B   17
        Impacts on the Natural Environment   17
        Impacts on Visitor Use   17
        Impacts on the Cultural Environment   17
    Alternative C   18
        Impacts on the Natural Environment   18
        Impacts on Visitor Use   18
        Impacts on the Cultural Environment   18

CONSULTATION AND COORDINATION   19

BIBLIOGRAPHY   21

PREPARERS   22

MAPS

Region   2

Vicinity   4

Existing Conditions   5

Alternative A Site Plan   13

PURPOSE OF AND NEED FOR THE ACTION

In 1979 a development concept plan (DCP) for the Giant Forest/Lodgepole area of Sequoia National Park was approved. It recommended a phased relocation of development from the sensitive sequoia groves in Giant Forest to more resilient environments. Major components of that DCP are to convert Giant Forest to a day use area; develop Clover Creek for visitor lodging and associated facilities, concession employee housing, and a new sewage treatment plant; develop Wolverton Corrals area for day use parking and transportation staging; provide a public transportation system linking developed areas; expand Dorst Creek campground for group camping; develop Red Fir for maintenance facilities and a sewage disposal sprayfield; and redesign the campground and employee community at Lodgepole.

One aspect of the plan is provision of additional visitor services at Lodgepole. The purpose of this environmental assessment is to evaluate three alternative plans for the area, with varying scales of development.

Previous planning efforts have offered different scales of development for a Lodgepole market. In 1973 the National Park Service approved a construction plan that included a market, a gift shop, fast food service, warehousing, and public laundromat and showers. The 1979 DCP also recognized a need for visitor services at Lodgepole and proposed a camper store (market) for construction in the area, without specifically identifying its functions. Currently, Guest Services Incorporated, the park concessioner, has proposed construction of a facility that would include all of the functions approved in 1973 and add a linen laundry and employee quarters. Because of Lodgepole's central location within Sequoia and Kings Canyon National Parks, warehousing and the linen laundry would serve the entire complex, thus providing a more efficient and economic operation.

This analysis of the impacts of the possible actions is intended to serve as a supplementary document to the 1979 Final Environmental Statement/Development Concept Plan (FES/DCP), Sequoia and Kings Canyon National Parks completed for the Giant Forest/Lodgepole area. For a complete discussion of the recommended actions and alternatives considered, reference can be made to that document, which is available from the office of the superintendent, Sequoia and Kings Canyon National Parks.

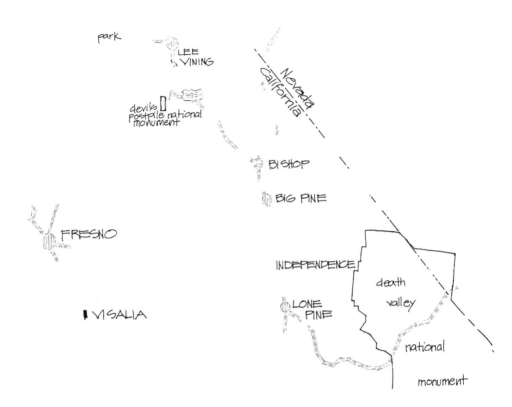

park

LEE
VINING

Nevada
California

devil's
postpile national
monument

BISHOP

BIG PINE

FRESNO

INDEPENDENCE

death
valley

VISALIA

LONE
PINE

national

monument

BSFIELD

to los angeles

REGION

SEQUOIA/KINGS CANYON NP/CALIFORNIA
UNITED STATES DEPARTMENT OF THE INTERIOR/
NATIONAL PARK SERVICE

NORTH

102|40067 B
DSC| DEC 81

AFFECTED ENVIRONMENT

EXISTING CONDITIONS

Lodgepole (see map) is one center of camping in the two park complex. Approximately 260 sites are located on 31 acres in the valley. Existing visitor services include a small camper store, visitor center, service station, and post office. A 3-acre paved surface adjacent to the camper store was constructed at the same time as Generals Highway. This paved surface is used for parking in summer and parking and recreational vehicle camping in winter. Hiking trails lead to Giant Forest and along the Marble Fork to Tokopah Falls.

Housing for NPS employees on the north side of the river occupies 12 acres. A 1-acre NPS maintenance facility is associated with this housing complex.

The Lodgepole water system was constructed in 1933 and substantially reconstructed in 1963. The present source of water for the Lodgepole area is Silliman Creek. Water treatment facilities consist of pressure filtration and chlorination. Water is stored in a 200,000-gallon underground reservoir.

A new sewage treatment plant is under construction near the Clover Creek development site to replace an inadequate facility for Lodgepole. A wastewater pipeline from Lodgepole to the treatment plant has been completed. The plant is being constructed to handle all of the Lodgepole wastewater and is designed to be enlarged to handle Clover Creek wastewater when lodging/restaurant facilities are moved to that location.

NATURAL ENVIRONMENT

Geology

Lodgepole is located in the glacially carved Tokopah Valley, through which the Marble Fork of the Kaweah River flows. The valley trends east/west, with an elevation of 6,720 feet at Lodgepole. Morainal deposits form slopes rising above the valley floor.

The Lodgepole area consists of granitic basement rock. Exposures of the original granodiorite complex can be seen in the Lodgepole/Clover Creek area. Glacial till deposits are scattered throughout the Lodgepole area.

Detailed information on the natural resources of the Lodgepole area is found in the 1979 FES/DCP. Material related to the proposal is repeated in this section.

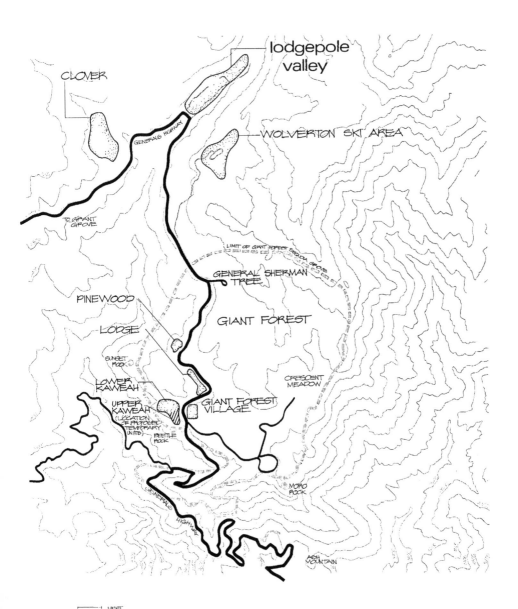

CLOVER

lodgepole
valley

WOLVERTON SKI AREA

GENERALS HIGHWAY

TO GRANT
GROVE

LIMIT OF GIANT FOREST SEQUOIA GROVE

GENERAL SHERMAN
TREE

PINEWOOD

GIANT FOREST

LODGE

SUNSET
ROCK

CRESCENT
MEADOW

LOWER
KAWEAH

UPPER
KAWEAH
(LOCATION
OF PROPOSED
TEMPORARY
UNITS)

GIANT FOREST
VILLAGE

BEETLE
ROCK

MORO
ROCK

GENERALS
HIGHWAY

ASH
MOUNTAIN

1 FEET
0   1600

VICINITY
lodgepole valley

SEQUOIA/KINGS CANYON NATIONAL PARKS
UNITED STATES DEPARTMENT OF THE INTERIOR/NATIONAL PARK SERVICE

NORTH

102 | 40 YL
DEC | JUL 82

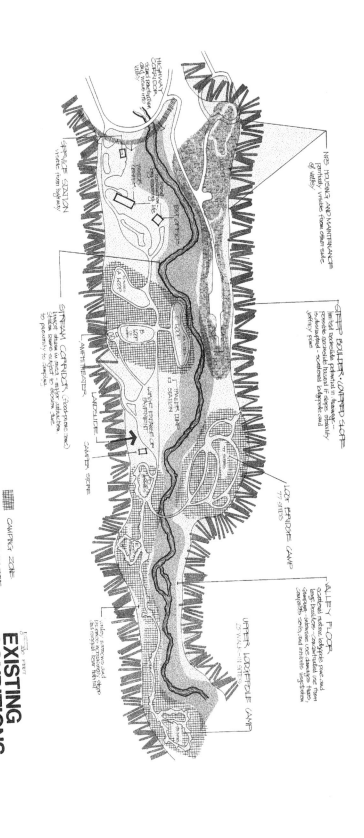

EXISTING
CONDITIONS
lodgepole valley

SEQUOIA/KINGS CANYON NATIONAL PARKS
UNITED STATES DEPARTMENT OF THE INTERIOR
NATIONAL PARK SERVICE

CAMPING ZONE

FLOOD-PRONE ZONE

HIGHWAY CORRIDOR
visual distraction and noise to most of the valley

NPS HOUSING AND MAINTENANCE
partially visible from other side of valley

SERVICE STATION
visible from highway

STEEP BOULDER-COVERED SLOPE
limited accessible potential in frontage - possible rockslide hazard if done stability is disrupted - scattered lodgepole and jeffrey pine

STREAM CORRIDOR (flood-prone zone)
lowest strata in area - major attraction, stream banks subject to erosion due to proximity to campsites

AMPHITHEATER

LANDSLIDE

CAMPER STORE

LOG BRIDGE CAMP
77 SITES

VALLEY FLOOR
scattered mature lodgepole pine and large boulders - compacted soil from campuse - intensive use damage from campuse, soils, and inhibits vegetation

UPPER LODGEPOLE CAMP
25 WALK-IN SITES

Soils

The Kaugh Shinn series soils are associated with and found adjacent to the Marble Fork of the river. Gefo series extend from the river corridor to the base of the valley slopes and occur on gently sloping glaciofluvial outwash deposited on top of older alluvium. Soil texture in the Gefo series is a gravelly coarse sandy loam with cobbles throughout the profile and some large boulders in the substream. In both series, a silica-cemented pan occurs at depths between 40 and 60 inches, but may be shallower or locally absent.

Water Resources

The Marble Fork runs through the Lodgepole area, and from its headwaters to Lodgepole it drains approximately 8,512 acres. Silliman Creek, which is west of Lodgepole and flows into the Marble Fork below Lodgepole, serves as the area's water source.

Water supply evalutations have been conducted for the Lodgepole/Clover Creek area, and a firm yield from Silliman Creek was determined to be 70 gallons per minute (gpm) or 100,800 gallons per day (gpd). The firm yield of the Marble Fork, a potential water source, was calculated to be 100 gpm or 144,000 gpd, as measured approximately 600 feet upstream from the easternmost campground at Lodgepole.

A brief survey of geohydrological characteristics was conducted, and potential groundwater yields from wells were determined to be low.

The Marble Fork has a history of flooding in the Lodgepole area. Annual spring floods from snowmelt rise approximately 5 feet above the summertime stream level. Midwinter floods, which are the largest, have damaged campsites within 100 feet of the stream. There has been no mapping done of the 100-year floodplain in the valley area.

Vegetation

At an elevation of 6,720 feet on south-facing slopes, lodgepole pine dominates the valley bottom. Much of the construction site has been altered by previous development and visitor use (paved parking area, trampling due to the location near the existing post office and parking facility), and the limited understory is composed primarily of saplings of the same species. A moist tall-grass meadow is located along the river between the post office and visitor center.

Wildlife

The Lodgepole area supports mixed conifer and brush wildlife habitats; riparian habitat is found in the Marble Fork corridor. The area adjoins good black bear habitat, providing some natural food resources.

Bears frequent the Lodgepole campground and continue to damage visitor property in their quest for food, despite a concerted effort to remove sources of unnatural sustenance.

The proposed development should not add new sources of unnatural food, nor increase the number and types of visitor contacts with problem bears.

Other commonly observed wildlife in the area includes chickaree, lodgepole chipmunk, long-eared bat, Stellers jay, mountain chickadee, white-headed woodpecker, and brown creeper. Golden eagles nest in the area.

Endangered or Threatened Species

No wildlife or plant species listed by the U.S. Fish and Wildlife Service (FWS) as threatened or endangered are known to currently occur in the Lodgepole study area (FWS, May 20, 1980). In addition, no candidate plant species occur in the area (FWS, Dec. 15, 1980).

Air Quality

The FES/DCP for Lodgepole indicates that the primary source of pollutants is highly populated areas outside the park. The pollutants are carried to the study site by air currents, and the immediate concentrations depend on meteorological conditions.

The main source of air pollutants within the park is from vehicular traffic on the Generals Highway. Increased vehicular traffic would cause the air quality in the region to deteriorate; however, pollution sources outside the park appear to be more significant than pollution generated within the park.

VISITOR USE AND EXPERIENCE

Visitation

The number of visitors to Sequoia and Kings Canyon totaled 1,877,500 in 1981. Generally, visitation increased until 1978, when the total declined. Since that time the numbers have been steadily increasing each year. Over 70 percent of the visits occur from June through September. Visitors to Lodgepole are primarily campers or people touring the visitor center and attending evening campfire programs.

Annual Visitation

Year	Sequoia	Kings Canyon	Total
1981	1,095,064	784,472	1,877,500
1980	862,800	823,800	1,686,600
1979	799,600	804,200	1,603,800

8

1978	973,400	869,900	1,843,300
1977	978,600	1,046,600	2,025,200
1976	1,040,575	1,127,902	2,168,477
1975	957,386	1,035,294	1,992,680
1974	686,940	1,224,400	1,911,340
1973	846,280	906,770	1,753,050
1972	869,600	1,058,040	1,927,640
1971	882,000	896,690	1,778,690
1970	875,670	1,018,990	1,894,660

Visitor Experience

Lodgepole, intended to be the primary center for camping, is a hub for backcountry use and draws those seeking an alpine experience. Its visitor center is a major focal point in the two parks. As many as 1,100 campers a day stay at Lodgepole during the peak visitor season. The minimal services available include a gas station and small store.

Scenic Quality

Lodgepole has the visual features of a "classic" glaciated valley corridor, and the Marble Fork is a prime attraction. The valley is comparatively level, dry terrain with scattered boulders and sparse vegetation. From many locations in the valley, visitors can find spectacular views of the High Sierra.

CULTURAL ENVIRONMENT

Prehistory

Prior to historic times, the Sequoia/Kings Canyon region was inhabited by the Western Mono, Yokuts, and Owens Valley Paiute native tribes (Steward 1935). Their subsistence was based primarily on hunting and gathering, which entailed seasonal migrations from permanent base camps to temporary camps at higher elevations. The park area was also utilized as a trade route by the Western Mono and the Owens Valley Paiute.

The Lodgepole area was surveyed for archeological resources in 1974 by the Institute of Archeological Research survey team. The survey area included a major portion of the Marble Fork of the Kaweah River from a few hundred feet west of the confluence of the Wolverton Creek complex. No archeological resources were discovered, and archeological clearance was recommended. The Western Archeological Center subsequently issued a series of clearances (SERI-296, SERI-297, SERI-298) in December 1977 covering the Lodgepole developed area. The specific site was again surveyed in the spring of 1982. Unconditional clearance was issued as a result of that most recent survey (037-82 SEKI, June 24, 1982).

History

Discovery of Giant Forest by non-Indians occurred in 1858. In that year a group of Yokuts living in the vicinity of Hospital Rock invited Hale Tharp to join them in a visit to their summer camps in the mountains. Tharp was eventually led to the Giant Forest plateau.

By the 1880s the indiscriminate harvest of sequoias caused preservation efforts to focus on withdrawing the groves from public domain. Those efforts culminated in congressional action in 1890 that established Sequoia National Park.

In compliance with Executive Order 11593 and section 106 of the National Historic Preservation Act, a thorough historic resources study, "Sequoia-Kings Canyon National Parks: A History of the Parks," was completed in 1975 by Dr. A. Berle Clemensen. The Marble Fork and Clover Creek bridges near Lodgepole are listed on the National Register.

ALTERNATIVES

In this assessment three alternatives are presented for consideration and review. They are restricted to the specific action to be implemented at Lodgepole, since other aspects of the approved plan for the Lodgepole area have not changed substantially. Reference can be made to the 1979 FES/DCP for a detailed discussion of the overall plan and its attendant impacts. For any of the three alternatives, utilities are available. Water is supplied from Silliman Creek, and wastewater will be treated at Clover Creek. A criterion for building would be to ensure architectural compatibility with existing buildings and scenic qualities.

ALTERNATIVE A--THE PROPOSED ACTION

Alternative A will allow Guest Services Incorporated to construct a visitor services complex that will include a market, gift shop, delicatessen, public showers, public laundry, linen laundry (for GSI lodging wthin the two parks), warehouse, and limited employee quarters on the second floor. The proposed location of the facility and its relationship to the existing buildings and circulation systems in Lodgepole are shown on the following site plan.

ALTERNATIVE B

Alternative B proposes construction of only a camper store, as recommended in the 1979 development concept plan

ALTERNATIVE C

This complex would include a smaller camper store, a gift shop, delicatessen, public showers and laundry, and warehouse. This alternative differs from A by not including a linen laundry and employee quarters and by scaling down the store. The National Park Service approved in 1973 a complex of this nature for construction by the concessioner, but it was not built. The location of this complex would be the same as in alternative A.

CONCESSION BUILDING
ELI/KITCHEN / GIFT SHOP
T/ SHOWERS
PKY / WAREHOUSE
APARTMENTS

ICE

CENTER

STATION

VISITOR CENTER PARKING
34 SPACES

TRAILER
PARKING
5 SPACES

SERVICE DOCK

EMPLOYEE PARKING
11 SPACES

TRAILER PARKING

BIKE PATH

CONCESSION PARK
62 SPACES

EXISTING
CAMPGROUND LOOP

CAMPGROUND →

KAWEAH RIVER

○ EXISTING TREE
⊙ PROPOSED TREE
⊙ CONIFER
◉ DECIDUOUS
▨ SHADE STRUCTURE

NPS

ALTERNATIVE A
SITE PLAN
lodgepole valley

SEQUOIA/KINGS CANYON NATIONAL PARKS
UNITED STATES DEPARTMENT OF THE INTERIOR /
NATIONAL PARK SERVICE

ENVIRONMENTAL CONSEQUENCES

CONSEQUENCES COMMON TO ALL ALTERNATIVES

Temporary impacts common to all alternatives relate principally to effects generated by construction activities. For example, soil compaction would result, causing an increase in runoff, and reduced infiltration Vegetation would be removed or disturbed in the immediate vicinity of the project. Wildlife would also be disturbed and displaced, regardless of the alternative implemented. Finally, air quality would be slightly degraded for the lifetime of the construction project by increased emissions and dust generated from construction vehicles. The primary difference between the alternatives would be the extent of the acreage affected. For alternative A, as much as 4 acres could be committed to the development of the facility, parking, and circulation system. The kinds and amount of impacts for alternative C would be essentially the same as for alternative A, including nearly the same amount of acreage. For alternative B, the camper store would commit approximately 1 acre to new development. The impact discussion is organized to provide a complete analysis of the expanded proposal of alternative A, followed by alternatives B and C. Wherever the impacts appear similar, alternatives B and C are referenced to the discussion for alternative A. It should be noted that differences between the three alternatives generally relate to the scale of development.

ALTERNATIVE A--THE PROPOSED ACTION

Impacts on the Natural Environment

Soils. The proposed facility will be located in an area of Shinn and Gefo series soils. Both series have been identified as having a high erosion potential and a moderate to high compaction potential. As stated previously, construction activities associated with site development will result in soil compaction and increased erosion potential in the short run. Long-range impacts expected on soils will occur primarily as a result of pedestrian and vehicular traffic generated by the new facility.

Water Resources. The construction-related impact of increased erosion potential will also temporarily degrade the water quality in the Marble Fork of the Kaweah River until the disturbed areas stabilize. Surface runoff will also increase from the structure and associated pavement.

Implementation of alternative A will also result in diversion of additional surface waters from Silliman Creek. The proposed facility with its expanded functions will require approximately 17,000 gpd during the visitor use season. This represents a withdrawal of approximately one-sixth of the firm yield of Silliman. The peak period of water diversion will occur in summer, the low-flow period of Silliman Creek. The direct effect of this water diversion includes lowered and/or altered populations of aquatic vertebrates and invertebrates. Riparian vegetation will be adversely affected. Groundwater levels dependent upon surface recharge will be decreased. Wastewater from the facility will be treated at the Clover Creek treatment plant. Therefore, effluent from the store and laundry is not expected to cause any significant impact on downstream aquatic resources.

Vegetation. The site selected for the facility already has been affected by development of campsites, roadways, parking areas, and the utility corridor. Understory vegetation is sparse; approximately 25 Jeffrey pines will be removed in order to accommodate the development.

Visitor use will have ongoing impacts on vegetation and indirect impacts on environmental conditions necessary for regeneration, concentrated around the building, parking lots, and roads. In all situations, plants will be trampled and soils eroded and compacted, creating poor conditions for regeneration. These effects will be largely mitigated by planting and irrigation. In the long run, these impacts might lead to reduced vegetation density as existing trees and understory die.

Wildlife. No recognized impacts will result except those discussed in the introduction. Loss of wildlife habitat and displacement of wildlife will be confined to the acreage required for the development and is negligible.

Air Quality. Because the major contribution to pollutants in the Lodgepole area is from external sources in California's Central Valley, the amount of traffic generated by the proposed facility will not cause significant deterioration in the air quality.

Impacts on Visitor Use

Services. In the current proposal, in addition to the area camper store, services including showers, laundry, gift shop, and fast food will be provided onsite. Additionally, noncamping functions including a warehouse, employee quarters, and linen laundry will be accommodated in the new facility. This will modify the Lodgepole experience to some degree, since Lodgepole was intended to be the primary center for camping in the original plan. However, implementation should not influence visitor use trends at Lodgepole to any significant degree.

Scenic Quality. The large complex will be readily visible and in close proximity to the flow of traffic to the campground and the visitor center. People coming to the visitor center or campground will have either of those experiences influenced by the presence of the market complex.

Visitor Experience. The visitor experience in the Lodgepole area will be altered by the development proposed in alternative A. More visitors will use the area for access to the showers, laundry, gift shop, and delicatessen, which will increase the amount of people contact, traffic, and parking congestion. The addition of the linen laundry and employee housing will increase vehicular traffic for servicing and supplies. However, the in-park linen laundry will eliminate three trips per week during peak season to the valley for linen service, thus reducing traffic on the Generals Highway.

Impacts on the Cultural Environment

No discernible impact on cultural resources will result from implementation of alternative A. The area was surveyed for archeological resources in 1974 and again in 1982 (037-82 SEKI). Clearance to proceed was obtained.

ALTERNATIVE B

Impacts on the Natural Environment

Soils. The impact on soils of the area would be the same as for alternative A but would affect only 1 acre.

Water Resources. The major difference in alternative B would be the water consumption of a camper store. It is estimated that the store alone would require only 3,000 gpd, thus the impact on Silliman Creek would be reduced because of the lower rate of diversion.

Vegetation. Same as alternative A, except reduced acreage affected.

Wildlife. Same as alternative A.

Air Quality. Same as alternative A.

Impacts on Visitor Use

Services. Under alternative B, only the services of a camper store would be offered at Lodgepole. Visitors desiring additional services would be required to travel to other areas of the two parks.

Scenic Quality. Construction of a camper store would result in a much lower-profile building than the complex proposed in alternative A. For visitors seeking a camping experience at Lodgepole, this facility would probably be in keeping with their expectations.

Visitor Experience. Compared to the complex, the camper store would have much less impact on the visitor experience. Fewer visitors would be drawn to the area, resulting in less visitor-to-visitor contact, traffic, and parking congestion. With no employee quarters or linen laundry, less traffic and parking congestion would be related to operation of the facility, but trucks would continue to carry linens to and from the valley on the Generals Highway.

Impacts on the Cultural Environment

Same as alternative A.

ALTERNATIVE C

Impacts on the Natural Environment

Impacts on the natural environment for this alternative are essentially the same as for alternative A. Less area would be impacted because the building would be smaller than in alternative A.

Impacts on Visitor Use

Impacts on visitor use would be similar to those identified for alternative A. The impacts associated with the linen laundry and employee quarters would not be present, but truck traffic would continue to and from the valley to provide for clean linens for the lodging facilities.

Impacts on the Cultural Environment

Same as alternative A.

CONSULTATION AND COORDINATION

Throughout the course of the original planning effort for the 1979 DCP, an extensive public involvement program was conducted. Discussions relevant to Lodgepole indicated strong support for camping in this area. Most members of the public expressed a desire for retention of camping at Lodgepole with some modifications, including separation of recreation vehicle campers and car campers to reduce conflicts. No specific discussions were held about the type or scale of services that are addressed in this document.

The current planning effort has involved a variety of interested parties in discussions on the changed proposal at Lodgepole. Included were national and regional representatives of the National Parks and Conservation Association, the Sierra Club, and the Audubon Society. The Resources Agency of the state of California was contacted to determine if they had any concerns with the proposal for Lodgepole. The Lodgepole postmaster was also informed of the proposed facility.

Copies of this environmental assessment will be sent to interested individuals and organizations for their comment and review.

BIBLIOGRAPHY

U.S. DEPARTMENT OF THE INTERIOR, FISH AND WILDLIFE SERVICE
1980   "Republication of Lists of Endangered and Threatened
            Species and Correction of Technical Errors in Final Rules."
            Federal Register.   Vol. 19, no. 99 and vol. 45, no. 242.

    1980   "Endangered and Threatened Wildlife and Plants: Review
                of Plant Taxa for Listing as Endangered or Threatened
                Species."   Federal Register.   Vol. 45, no. 242.

U.S. DEPARTMENT.OF THE INTERIOR, NATIONAL PARK SERVICE
1975   "Sequoia-Kings Canyon National Parks: A History of the
            Parks," by A. B. Clemensen.   Denver: Denver Service
            Center.

    1979   Final Environmental Statement/Development Concept Plan,
                Sequoia and Kings Canyon National Parks, California.
                Denver: Denver Service Center.

DENVER SERVICE CENTER

Cam Hugie   Project Manager

John Brooks   Environmental Specialist

John Ochsner   Landscape Architect

Bill Koning   Economist

John Latschar   Historian

SEQUOIA/KINGS CANYON NATIONAL PARKS

Boyd Evison   Superintendent

John Palmer   Chief Naturalist

Ken Backmeyer   Chief of Maintenance

Marv Jensen   Management Assistant

As the nation's principal conservation agency, the Department of the Interior has basic responsibilities to protect and conserve our land and water, energy and minerals, fish and wildlife, parks and recreation areas, and to ensure the wise use of all these resources. The department also has major responsibility for American Indian reservation communities and for people who live in island territories under U.S. administration.

Publication services were provided by the graphics staff of the Denver Service Center.   NPS 1930

Lightning Source UK Ltd.
Milton Keynes UK
UKHW010606120219
337137UK00007B/1572/P